the magic my body becomes

**ETEL ADNAN
POETRY SERIES**

Edited by
Hayan Charara and Fady Joudah

the magic my body becomes

POEMS BY JESS RIZKALLAH

The University of Arkansas Press
Fayetteville
2017

ISBN: 978-1-68226-040-1
e-ISBN: 978-1-61075-619-8

21 20 19   5 4 3

Designed by Liz Lester

⊗ The paper used in this publication meets the minimum requirements
of the American National Standard for Permanence of Paper
for Printed Library Materials Z39.48-1984.

Library of Congress Control Number: 2017941838

Supported in part by the King Fahd Center for Middle East Studies
at the University of Arkansas and Radius of Arab American Writers.

SERIES EDITORS' PREFACE

Among the things the lyric attempts to address and negotiate is the contemporary state of diction, of language, both spoken and sung. In poetry, this manifests in registers that amalgamate the living history and the canon of a particular language. In this case, we mean English and the "minor" Englishes that inform, prop, and expand it. At its best the lyric elicits a new horizon for and within its medium.

Jess Rizkallah's ambitious dance between the spoken word, or oral poetics, and the exegesis of the written give her debut collection its remarkable sheen. In her lyric, it's hard not to marvel at the balancing act, risky at times, between the intensity of abandon and that of silence. Her poems alternate between deliberate syntactical wildness (from which a delectable ephemerality results) and stunning precision. "I was born an arm with a hand at both ends/holding a knife." In fact, the deeper one gets into the book, the more one encounters an archeology that the poet's brushstrokes reveal: "my thighs meet each other like a prayer. I've got rosary beads/where bikes would have chains." The memorable moments are plentiful yet the poet reminds us: "these are not gifts, they're buried artifacts."

The shorter poems, the "Ghada says" sequence and the "aphorisms," for example, illustrate these finds. But many of the longer poems, especially the prose poems, are prime examples of her full range. The title alone of "*deir al qamar* means *convent of the moon* and it's all i think about" broadcasts the adventure. And the first few lines (and the entire poem, of course) continue it, surprising us with a humor driven to the bare teeth of sentimentality: "i wanna marriage aziz ansari / because he says clever things on the internet / and i want to marriage the tallest mountain on the planet because it's the closest one to the moon." Here and elsewhere, the result is a tug-of-war between restlessness and restraint, yes, but also the poet's various tongues, senses, and modes of understanding: "things will get complicated," the poet says, and they do.

Quips and tenderness give way to violence and tragedy, to uncompromising realities that, in turn, revert to wisecracks and empathy. "I realized this at 23" gathers so much of the manuscript in a well-packed suitcase containing many of Rizkallah's concerns: womanhood, in its Arabic and American dialogue; origins and roots (which clash in her last name, where even God for a Christian Arab doesn't escape America's flinch toward erasure); the insistence on objectivity through the world of things, the things in the world: toothpaste and a child's crayons.

There's no skirting around this: all literature, if not all art, is a grappling with identity in its particular locale and private domain. Whether identity is the founder or disintegration of sovereignty, and whether a cat chases its tail in perpetuity or in spurts, the means and perception of the self in question are as singular and plural as they're vetted by the congress of the multicultural. Or as Rizkallah aptly puts it: "this is how we compete/with the silence that wants to take us.

In America, there is a default mode about what makes a poet "limited" to the political or to the "ethnic." Often the default mode is a question of race but also of nationalism: our inverse Angel of History who looks away from the wreckage while flying full force into it. Rizkallah's concern with her body as her own and as product of "ways of seeing"; her struggle with god, her Christian god and her Arabic self as goddess; her struggle with the liminality of utterance; her specific Lebanese Maronite background and its recent history in Lebanon's civil war, which marks her family narrative and her memory of the world; her insistence on resisting her own American violence in general and against a people she belongs to as a Christian; the power this delivers to a liberal conversation about Muslims in America; all this ruptures absence in the name of what's better:

> I was named a miracle   still, they wait
> for something greater.

Literature is necessarily a grappling with expression, with what to reveal, what to bring attention to, which voices make agency possible. Some poets never really take this risk. Others have no choice. About this,

Rizkallah has a "Ghada says," which we want to imagine she kept close to her while writing these poems, if not posted on a wall or window where she writes, then in the back of her mind as a constant echo, kindling the fire:

why are you closing the curtain   let them stare.

Hayan Charara
Fady Joudah

ACKNOWLEDGMENTS

For Ghada, Moni, Milad, Antoinette, Najat, Afif, Mounir, Sasha, Jacob. You are my moons. I look to you and the poems find me. All my loving aunts, uncles, and family between America, Lebanon, and anywhere else you have landed. Your stories live in my heart every day. My cousins Dalia, Danny, Dylan, Mandy, Samo, Chadi, Rachel, Paco, Tia, Nado, Lilo, Johnny, Chrissy, Matthew, Anthony: thank you for the Pokémon battles, for staying outside way past when the streetlights came on, and for encouraging me to stay weird.

Cat and Ramy, nocturnal breakfast club of my heart. Izzy, Kate, Marisa, my sisterlings.

My Pizza Pi Press / intergalactic-whale coven: Cassandra de Alba, Tiffany Mallery, Melissa Lozada-Oliva, Josh Cornillon, Emmanuel Oppong-Yeboah.

Gratitude to Clara Ronderos for seeing me when I felt invisible and for refusing anything less than my best work. Chris Clark, Aaron Smith, Amanda McGregor, John Sullivan, Karen Fitzgerald, Karen Everette, Bud Jennings, Matthew Rohrer, Dave Bondar, Megan Fernandes, Michael Lambert, Jaswinder Bolina, Mary Beth Donovan, Laurie Miller Voke, for their encouragement over the years as educators, mentors, and friends.

My sunflowers: Aleyda Mendoza, Ashley Simmons, Deirdre Douglas, Lexi Halaby, Damien Quinter, Nouf Alsharif, Antoinette Feghali, Rony Fakhry, Shaena Baddour, Momo Elhout, Nebal Al-Taweel, Mikhail Johnson, Katy Denault, Mel Proulx, Kelso Fox, Hannah Rego, Ali Russo, Alina MacLean, Danielle Maio, Lindsay Blevins, Ian Ljutich, Jen Epervary, Julia Messier, Tynan Byrne, Adam Mooney, Erin Kelly, Megan Moyles, Dylan Gibson, Sarah Croughwell, Nathan Coney, Carol Glynn, Abbie Levesque, Amaryllis Hager, Kylie Bleau, Noelle BuAbbud, Cassandra Abou-Farah, Kevin Menasco, Tyler Roberge, Stacia Brezinski, Emily Welden, Sara Mae Henke,

Georgina Arroyo, Perpetua Charles, Elizabeth Hajjar, Derek Kunze, Molly Mulligan, Noor Wafai, Jared Blouin, Jack Ardery, Paige Chaplin, Taylor Liljegren, Ray Cohen, Ramon Hernandez, Judy Chong, Zachary Najarian-Najafi, Rowan K, Shem Tane, Tim Lavin

Haboubati, Marwa Helal, George Abraham, Safia Elhillo, Noor Jaber, Nader Helmy, Adam Hamze, Randa Jarrar, Amir Safi, Hazem Fahmy, Ragheb Khuja, and all the cousins of the MENAspora. Long live the groupchat.

Thank you endlessly to Boston and its creative communities, NorthBeast, and especially Cantab. Thank you to all the invisible forces that allow me to orbit such wonders as Simone Beaubien, Bobby Crawford, Sam Rush, McKendy Fils-Aime, RebeccaLynn Gualtieri, JR Mahung, Sophia Holtz, Emily Carroll, Josh Elbaum, Emily O'Neill, Hanif Willis-Abdurraqib, Sean Patrick Mulroy, Nora Meiners, Zeke Russell, Emily Eastman, Andy Locke, Jonathan Mendoza, Porsha Olayiwola, Janae Johnson, Ellyn Touchette, Ed Wilkinson, Kieran Collier, Manvir Singh, Ryan Carson, Allison Trujillo, Adam Stone, Laura Willis-Abdurraqib, Franny Choi, Kye Noelle, Angelica Maria Aguilera, Rachel Sahlein, Chloé Cunha, Evan Cutts, John Pinkham, Oompa, Austin Hendricks, Andrew Campana, Ariel Baker-Gibbs, Gemma Cooper-Novack, Anna Binkovitz, Meaghan Ford, Zenaida Peterson, Fisayo Adeyeye, Cassandra Euphrat-Weston, Henri Garrison, Julian David Randall, Aria Aber, Diannely Antigua, Kevin Devine, Lady Lamb, the people at DMChoir, MICExpo, Lesley University, and everyone else who I am only momentarily forgetting but whose art, activism, and presence have changed my life.

My NYU CWP family, who shift my pen in vital ways and make New York into a home. RAWI and University of Arkansas Press for making my dream come true. Fady and Hayan for seeing me, believing me, trusting me, and looking out for me.

Jido, for telling me about the river. For sending me birds. For showing me how poems emerge in the way sunlight shifts over hands resting on a table. What a gift you still are, even now, as you live in that light.

I love you all.

Earlier versions of some of these poems have appeared in *NAILED*, *Ant vs. Whale*, *Drunk in a Midnight Choir*, *Button Poetry*, *Slam Find*, *Spoken & Sung*, *HEArt Journal*, *Word Riot*, *Inferior Planets*, *Jaffat El Aqlam*, *Voicemail Poems*, *Mizna*, *Wyvern*, *Sukoon*, and *Commonthought*.

"a voice takes hold of the bottom of my feet, moves up along my legs,
stops at my knees and bends them slowly, slides like a sail
on the Nile along my spine and bursts into millions
of cells of my brain. I am a magic box."

—ETEL ADNAN

CONTENTS

Ghada says   3

take a left here   4

deir al qamar means *convent of the moon*
and it's all i think about   5

Ghada says   6

bop bop   7

my assignment is to "draw chaos"   8

Ghada says   9

on practicing my arabic   10

if teta never had to leave lebanon i wonder
if she would make preserves   11

white man says to my brown father   13

I realized this at 23:   14

aphorisms for lonely arabs   15

you got way too excited about annihilation
before the cosmic folk show   16

Sin el Fil, Lebanon   17

when they ask me who i pray to   20

Ghada says   22

poem as my dad   23

the backroads   25

she'll make a husband so happy one day   26

my other mouth   27 fine then   28

Ghada says   29

tbh i've got more things to say about hair
than i have hair   30

sometimes i feel like my own life would
never pass the bechdel test   31

when daughters are not enough   33

there goes the family   35

Ghada says   36

"i'll bury you"   37

Ghada says   38

i am always carrying boxes   39

dream log   40

Ghada says   42

something uglier than a flower   43

my thighs could kill a man   45

give me the flute & sing   46

ahwak   47

notepad fragments   48

origin story   50

Ghada says   52

i am a garden of bones but don't call me
a cemetery   53

Notes   55

the magic my body becomes

Ghada says

fresh lemons always.
not that bottled shit.

when you're halving the lemons to juice them, cut
a cross into the middle with the tip of the knife

this is how it's done in the mountains.

take a left here

there's something wrong with the lungs in my family.
they absorb the wind but can never take the shock.

broken chimes, they wait for us
to activate them
to send in flares

for us to be helpless
buoys in the storm.

our roots began by the sea
took their first steps

the foam borrowed salt from earth
to cake the brine

built our parts there and ran
before the birth of war.

the mediterranean does not forget,
only lets me think myself a vessel
on higher ground

until the sea feels like snatching my body back.

i climb mountains with monasteries
named for the moon

and the moon whispers
a secret to the tides   There. That's The Beginning.

deir al qamar means *convent of the moon* and it's all i think about

i wanna marriage aziz ansari / because he says clever things on the internet / and i want to marriage the tallest mountain on the planet because it's the closest one to the moon / but i wanna use it to get to the moon / i want to run away with the moon / but things will get complicated, i'll still be in love with the mountain / because some part of you loves everyone you've ever loved even if you don't love them anymore / i'll always love the mountain / because it's seen me naked with the lights on / in a past life we were newsies / getting lost on backstreets / dropping skin cells / before that, neighbors / i'd leave a cup of soup on his doorstep whenever the taragon was extra crisp / every time it rained i'd find a different piece of colored glass to glue into my skin / then i was a window / left him to throw myself at the sun / rode the coattails of bullet cases / the sun shrapneled me into my mother's garden / she found me thirty years later / nestled between the tomatoes / carried me in her seeds / would learn me how to love / before that the mountain was my wife and i was a bad husband / have you ever used stained glass for evil / then watched it escape / my skin gets caught on the lint of my scarf / when it screams red / when it swallows the chemicals / while i scrub dishes made of the prelude to everything i'm going to ruin / and it burns

Ghada says

your spine
is a river
the rest of
you will always
return to.

bop bop

jido is sick and my sister isn't eating and i found out that nothing lives inside the belly of an elephant except for the love it swallows when the love doesn't want to swallow it back. but it still makes their hair grow. the brain is a stop sign now. it's nickels against cardboard when i'm sad. it's the moon. you ever seen a ghost? you ever dreamed about soda-can people? they live in the dregs of civil war, in the aftermath of the burp. in the trail of history's nails against its own wrists, trenches for alternate timelines. i don't know jack but jack knew my mom. he died at 18, swallowed by love but not before he swallowed gunfire. megafauna of the chest: nickels shooting out of the body. blood cells arranging into elephant before becoming confetti against olive trees. scarlet pillbugs. all tusk through his red t-shirt. he hugs my mother as she chops parsley and he doesn't know that i know he could've been my father, and he wants to be, but i already have a father. i had a dream about fevers once. buttons the size of trees, futures peeking through the threadholes. eyes opening like mouths. my sister still not eating, nothing lives inside her belly and jido asked me about the condition attached to the frontal lobe as we juggle our dreams. he asked me what i saw in mine. i didn't tell him i saw him there as a child, but not quite. he looked more like a ghazal with fig trees for arms and himself as a child swinging from the branches. but i just told him about the moon full of bees bouncing against the earth like your eye against a first love's eye. he told me his brain is an upside-down chair when he has a fever. he has a fever. all tusk, like a streetlight.

my assignment is to "draw chaos"

micron pen like a hatchet overtaking the ivory i can't reach.
it's somewhere between my lungs from the first time someone really left.
it's what chaos tries to force out with smoke. three fires in one week.
a car bursting into flames outside my window. oxygen tank missing a beep.
scripture in the deviation of wood on the mantel.

my assignment is to draw blood   can't find it   i graze my arm
against the espresso machine when i try pulling shots fast enough but
my skin doesn't know how to talk about god

it has all these locks i'm afraid to pick.   sunspots that could return me
to Apollo himself so i pretend my own skin is god and I wait for the bus
i'm always waiting for the bus.

my sister was hit by a car but she doesn't talk about god
just pulls into the saint lucy's parking lot at the 2 pm bells
"i love that noise," she says. "no, that sound."

i can't hear it. my ears, always ringing. yesterday for five minutes
he spoke to her by my name   then she called me, let the phone ring twice
before hanging up.

whenever it comes, she is the canary before the air runs out.

Ghada says

here's how you do it   how you practice
your arabi: you pretend you're talking to god.
every night. ask him to spare you
by sparing those you tuck inside
for safekeeping.

on practicing my arabic

i fumble with the prayers i found baking
in the hot tar of my mother's womb when
she couldn't seal it in time for my arrival.

i know that the tongue forms first
if the tongue was ever something formed,
not found   and not ever really mine,
always a fractured leaf   or ripped out
throat of a warda, and always thorns.
of course. the opposite of an echo.
sharpness wanting to be flesh
but tearing flesh in its attempt.

this language
already a pearl, will never trust
me with a qasida. it doesn't
need my love.

if teta never had to leave lebanon
i wonder if she would make preserves

1.

i could stop calling the middle east the Middle East
i could call it Mediterranean or kitchen counter in the sunlight,
geckos napping in the window sill, parsley straining in the sink
i could call it abdelhalim hafez on the radio, tuning my mother's heart
teta's apples becoming vinegar under the sink
jido swallowing the moon every morning

but the collection of small miracles i like to call home is just the pinking skin
around a scab where once the earth was a mouth laughing like lutes and molasses.

why would i call this jagged wound a birthmark?

2.

they tell me to *be less Poetry* about my rage
also to be less poetry in my poetry   never let the poem know I'm talking
about it, *never let it know where you are*   *what it is, don't talk*
about writing. never talk   *about writing*   this is a game to play
while your people burn. today in the sun   tomorrow too
the next day: leather on the tectonic hot plate under the tongue
under the the pen drawing new lines where the earth was already wrinkled.

3.

they call the zig-zagged eastern border between Jordan and Saudi Arabia
Winston's Hiccup. Churchill once boasted of his liquid lunch,
of creating Jordan with a stroke of the pen one Sunday afternoon in Cairo

they tell me to be less phantoms wielding scalpels about it
less filling   but more cavity over the already drilled down
DNA that i speak   they tell me to just fucking say it

the nothing left to say   the mountains struggling to breathe
abdelhalim hafez, his heart stuck in the static's throat
the overwhelming twitch of the fingers
into a fist.

4.

sometimes there is only the bubble on the job applications
where you fill in a circle because you're working hard   you're a good
            American today

you get to be white   as long as you're behaving   but you're a liar
when they wound you   and stupid when you're sleeping.

never forget   you are the earth's oldest apples.

white man says to my brown father

go blow up your own country
i'm not buying a car from you

fires my father   replaces him
with another white man   let's say   tom
          or ted   maybe richard
and it's the first time i hear my father cry.

my grandmother says a hail mary
& he smashes the statuette of white jesus.

we still bring it with us when we move.

I realized this at 23:

Aladdin was supposed to be my brother.
Jasmine: me, except
all convex hourglass waist
i only ever saw in the squeeze of my toothpaste tube,
white solvent in my mouth.

my last name part REDACTED, part not
and when my ball goes into the street,
no American soldier's boot to rewrite me
into sweet prologue before the terror they will create
in the beginning of movies for little boys
who look like my cousin.

he sends me crayon drawings
of himself trapped inside bubbles
where no one can reach him.

aphorisms for lonely arabs

they will call you forked tongue.   let them.

swallow your blood and bare your teeth, they are seeds.

you are made of rings, ancient
you have always been here

what is a field of weeds to an entire ecosystem?

it's true, the forests often go up in smoke
the cedars are dying off
and drones live in the sky—

a splinter in the paw of a lion buys us time.

there must be a bush, burning patiently to lead us home.

you got way too excited about annihilation
before the cosmic folk show

there's a familiar red edge to things, everything is a curvature
of investment. even the follicles enflame,
    civil wars trying to escape from the sponge of us—
my body cultivates a forest of DNA i forget when i unboard an airplane
have i ever really lived if i've never jumped from a helicopter
or eaten cereal from the floor? pardon me
        maybe i'm always trying
to be the creak instead of the motion—

one night, he said:
    "one day, thousands of cultures will be gone, dying
    off all the time. always. and what's so wrong about that?"

and my words right to
left like smoke.
Kannoubine on fire in my throat
(that holy valley, its cavities my maronite ancestors climbed inside of)
(i wonder if i'm a traitor)
(if my mouth is just another genocide)
(my lexicon militiamen from the south)

i am foaming from
the second language
i learned when I say

"well i guess that's something, isn't it."

Sin el Fil, Lebanon

*

i asked her to tell me about the elephants

she used to live in one of their teeth
boroughed into beirut like a forgotten cavity
where her mother had cancer and her dog ran into traffic
the year before she married.

i asked her about the curve of the tusk at the base
of their home, and she said they huddled, three days,
bricks for pillows, sirens replacing birds   fingers coming through
the ground for the ankles not yet twisted by the rubble

the next day, they made for america,
the ivory still in the basement
cocooned by a silk curtain.

**

i asked him about the beginning of the war

he told me about the people walking over
broken glass.   everyone in the city
some sort of Jesus, with shards of what would
one day floss the Mediterranean
getting caught in their heels.

his first and only pet was a german shephard.
rin tin tin, a name like three sharpened teeth in a row

a bite   a mark made above the boot coming down
a heel too soft to know its own flesh.

***

he told me about mortality's breath
the matted fur between his children's arms
the organs like disintegrating pottery
when the militia fed his dog shrapnel.

he whimpered at the door til he was found,
abdomen giving way to scarlet fingers
red sea parted by his tongue and the final heave
before his body became a prophecy
for every cedar and every person
every cedar lives inside of.

** * *

as boston thaws over the morning dog walkers, i count all the ways
i have come to understand the distance my family keeps.

                    when enough homes collapse into mines,
                    anything close enough to lick your
                    wounds will sound like a canary.

*   *   ***

she asks me why i love the elephants
even though i can never hold them.

i tell her about the toenails and teeth, the tusks
and their bones, like these stories

they're something to know from afar,
to watch die from afar, leaving behind
their bodies as shelter.

i ask her how many years it would take to visit each
grave the past filled to bring me here. she tells me
that each day i am here is a flower left at a different stone.

when they ask me who i pray to

i say patron saint of the gap in my mother's front teeth

i say patron saint of the long-lost gap in my teeth, who took it back
but left me with a whistle. a reminder of the resemblance
i let myself forget.

i say patron saint of my grandfather's forehead,
who whispers about the heart on fire
under formaldehyde & earth.

patron saint of my sister's bitten nails that never catch dirt when she lays
flowers at the base of a stone that took five months to arrive because
no one else came around.

saint of the lemon tree his father put there
saint of the ripest tomatoes
saint of the shrapneled kitchen tile their baby feet slapped
saint of the blue peaks by the ocean where we began
saint of the way we say *what* again
and again as plea, as demand.

i know there are saints of lights not written about.
saints of walking sticks falling against floors not holy.
the saint of the self as god when god has done enough
to be reshelved and left dusty.

when they ask me, i say patron saint of teta's hands.
small hands that beaded and embroidered
and kneaded and carried and learned the alphabet.
a for apple. b for box. c for candle.
d for dog. d for death. d for dirt
under the nails. a hard day's work   a picture frame
and his cold wedding band.   this is how we compete
with the silence that wants to take us.

Ghada says

no one on this earth is as important as a sister
no man on this earth is owed any part of you
no man speaks to any daughter of mine like that

poem as my dad

you can't just say *Fuck Columbus* or *Fuck the Police*
don't scare me with what they'll do to you when they
pass over the white of your skin to who your parents are
don't let them notice your last name.

but never forget where you are from. the wooden ships.
never forget your last name. until you are married.
then forget.

you will always be my daughter. you look just like me.
you are me, like i threw up whatever made me half golden.
look at your eyes. those lashes. they're mine too.

take care of that hair on your face.
don't sit like that. cross your legs.
but not in church.
why don't you go to church anymore?

i don't want anyone to think you want anything from them
shame on them, but do pull up your shirt   hey now don't talk
about these things. these things about bodies. these things
about this new age. don't be such an american.
don't forget where you're from.

remember where you are.
there is one eye on you at all times, looking
for a furrowed brow. its resting stitch.
that unrelenting crosshatch. the twitching fist

behind your eyes.   chin high. it's okay,
let them think you too proud, they think pride harms us,
but it keeps us here. keeps us tearing our home country apart.
keeps us safe here.   don't let them *You People* you
they try to *You People* me on the phone when they
hear the sun clench its jaw in my tongue, I hang up on them,
no one hangs up on me. your mother hangs up on me.

listen, just tell me who you really are
just be my daughter, just tell me
what i need to know.

the backroads

my little sister tells me that a donut will make me happier
than any man ever will   and suddenly i am all laughter, lipstick
and then rage as we talk about
the daughterness of us.   open sunroof on a winter night,
but we came from the womb of a woman who
stays close to the eye of the storm
in herself
          our bodies follow suit. we are stone cold, we are bitches
we don't have much in common but this. it is enough
to be everything.

          i watch her peel the asphalt back. she flicks the road like a wrist,
hand tuned to the rosary swinging from her rearview mirror
hand flickering in and out of a fist   and now she is staring down
a red light.
          talking about a man who tried to tuck her
into a mountain once, tried to tell her when and where to avalanche
and how to do it quieter
          so she's got no time for white boys   no time
for beirut boys   no time
for anyone who tells her what to do

she is all eyebrows and incense
she is all ghost of the woman
who stared down the barrel of a gun
when the militia came for her

the man who gets to tell me what to do
          hasn't been born yet. he never will be.

she'll make a husband so happy one day

sometimes no one will ask you for your name.
they'll just call you   shlike

                sharmuta

                t'obrini

                habibi

                      farhet l'aris

my other mouth

i don't know what sort of music my other mouth whistles.
i'm not sure we can harmonize.
we don't talk.
just meet by the moon sometimes.
writhe because it tells me so: tangerines on fire.
a burnt persimmon.

and my uterus a tongue. its breath all fever.
my crossed legs, a clenched windchime.
i am shedding three months' worth of lining
and the fine sand of what used to be glass,
ripe from an angry jaw
these bones fit for a nest of gum
and fingernails. always snaps shut
before the murder hatches.

i forget every name i had picked out.
i grind my teeth down to nothing while i sleep.
i swallow the wrong potions
i thank the shadows on my wall.

once, as a child, i woke up before anyone else in the house:
looked out the window to find the yard covered in crows.
every blade of grass. every tree branch.
my mother's car. no clouds. no sun.
no witnesses. just black feathers.
beaks aimed at the sky. all of them still.
then at once, all of them gone.

fine then

call me monster   hairy monster, though   listen,
i'm not trying to be a suitable mate
just invisible

all these white boys pointing out my tail
all these ghosts on my tail
all this tail, they're mad

crazy bitch. hairy bitch.
quiet bitch. nice bitch.
fuckin bitch.   all fangs in the night, make no mistake.

Ghada says

why are you closing the curtain   let them stare

tbh i've got more things to say about hair than i have hair

if an arab girl caves into the forest of her body
is she the tree or the ax or is she the space between?

how easy it would be to steal into the kitchen after dark
into the third drawer. quick. painless.
the way mama parted the dough for the m'naaeech.
I fell asleep the way my claw marks faded,
but that memory didn't.

did you know even the collarbones can be hairy.
my own have caught my father's tears once then twice
& i can't tend to this murky aquarium without at least
mentioning the magic my body became:
i keep tender creatures safe.

when rabbits climb out of the mouths of prophets
the hairs on my stomach perk their ears
but my body already knows the past, picked the olives
then stripped the bark   save for these splinters
the sun has fashioned into a mane.

sometimes i am afraid these hairs are all i have left
but i still feel myself growing   all rings around
a muffled seed, its hum that never stopped
do you hear it?

sometimes i feel like my own life
would never pass the bechdel test

the eyeballs smeared into my thighs. and my proclamations of
pee all over everything they love / i will pee all over everything they love

they "love" too hard:
> acid to the face at the refusal of this love
>> the mutilation of where he thinks his love is stored
>> if she doesn't open her legs to welcome him   home

hang this on your wall / click share / we can talk
about stories claimed / how they become abdomens
over maps where western feminism runs its fingers
where it stores the Other under its nails / calls it dirt.   cleans it out
with the tip of the pen cap   to make everything white again

i keep talking about bike chains for arms. shank you with my collarbone.
          evolution being sick of the shit, turning fingers into keys. and
still these are only skewers   *whoa there*   nothing to find inside
yourself, sweetie. never forced entries just your fault for not locking up.
for spares laying around. in the glint of teeth under the streetlight.

and then me and my sister talk about our futures. how we can only pass
Lebanese citizenship to our children if we marry Lebanese men. i once
saw a Lebanese man drag his wife from the car by the hair.   i once
saw an American man do the same. the only difference was the Lifetime

logo in the corner.   the roll of the window rising / the flip of the
channel switching.
we are all silent in the wrong places.

my sister is never silent:
          the night she turns 18 i tell her to watch out for
                    that one there, his teeth,
his jawline a knife, a metaphor incomplete without her—she laughs,
burns him with her wit and he retreats   later someone will tell the
other girl that *good boys will be boys* and suddenly
my sister is every woman

a psychic tells me what i know:
          she sees purple. knows he is on my mind, tells me that i still
wonder if he ever loved me,   yes this is true yes him only yes i
was in love i guess yes he makes me want to die   inside always /
my insides his   kneecaps at every corner.   always seems to be
          a two-women vignette about these men.

there are days when i feel like: my own life will never have a man
                    turning my heart
          or my tongue   into a shadow with his name

when daughters are not enough

your sons are never collected when they spill shit
so we step around them, their shadows
resolute. like cedar. biblical. like cedar.
insects chewing at the roots. like cedar.

& left behind, here we are. exposed
not golden in the nakedness of day,
just naked, undeserving
of the day we fell here.

you see, the light only hits us right siphoned through
what the branches decide to grant us.
no fruits overhead. just rivers
of sap, our sticky fingers.

do we get to be the trees,
or do we just choose from them
the switch for the hand that
reminds us of this?

in this family: no son, so loud
in his not-thereness.
his inheritance lives on
somewhere inside my father
a locked door leading
to a room behind the resting stitch
above the glare, the twitching fist behind the eyes

this thin-lipped face like mine
that no son will ever know like i know.

but i'm one of the lucky ones.
i get to choose.

i get to watch the light hit whoever he is
just right   like it's not just reaching
through his branches
looking for me.

there goes the family

" . . . the double ducats, stol'n by the daughter!
and jewels—two stones, two rich and precious stones!
Justice! find the girl!"

—*Merchant of Venice*

Rizkallah   meaning: fortune of god   and my god

they think I'm going to give that back.

Ghada says

never leave the pan in the sink after making eggs
the smell lives in your nostrils if you leave
the invitation marinating.

"i'll bury you"

the taste of a wooden spoon against your mouth
becomes the frame of reference for every toothache

makes the jokes on popsicle sticks not funny anymore,
their splinters between your teeth will want to be part
of the ocean, salt leaking into your speech.

a toothpick once soldiered itself into my heel, half-mast
mistook my pulse for a sea shanty, expanded under hot water
before my mother ripped it out with tweezers and i screamed
at the molten crush throbbing from my step.

it had been discarded in the rug when my father
was finished picking the meat from his teeth.
his toothpick, driftwood   my spit, dead sea
percussion collected   in the way i talk
in all the splinters i've swallowed   i've been
burying things my whole life

the wooden spoon in the yard, i did it.
i wasn't supposed to   but it reemerged
as Jido's summer tomatoes

what was once the corpse of discipline
giving itself to the earth.

Ghada says

don't think you can fix anyone
if they prick you   every
                           single
                           time
the light hits them harshly,
it will always hurt.

i am always carrying boxes

i'm reading a book about medical records, phosphenes pressed between
pages like flowers my mom picked in the mountains on her way to school
before the jasmine stopped growing and she had to take a different path.
i can't stop thinking about my teeth, bulbs waiting to sprout when my
words figure out how to be spring and i'm really into almonds lately. really
into sleeping on the floor by my bed, i want to give my cells shorter jumps
before they hit the ground. i want them alive when they whisper names
of everyone they've met into the hardwood. the syllables will live here
long after i don't and soon i won't. i saw ian at work the other day for the
first time in months. or maybe a year. he wrote his number on a napkin i
put in my back pocket and then it fell out or i blew my nose or some shit
i don't know i don't remember but i'm not affected by that loss. four years
ago his voice was the sound of rain and i was asphalt cracking open, weeds
bursting from the silent shriek of me. my wrist will always remember the
feel of its neck between his nails as he showed me the way ink makes an
entrance & never leaves & i'm not one for the rough stuff but there are
certain types of pain i think about as i think about a collarbone in shadow
or the way the sun that one time let me see its outline then let me keep
my vision

dream log

#1

I'm with my squad. I don't actually know where they are.
There is cake everywhere. I keep swiping frosting on my fingers
when no one is watching.
There is no one watching.
There is always someone watching.

#2

I'm in a room-sized raisin with
windows beaming in sunlight
& sparrows are singing on the sills.
There is a photo of my grandfather on the wall
and George is standing behind me, nodding and smiling

we discuss the
the microscopic:
our cavities as excavation sites
for the trauma that isn't ours
but brought us here

#3

I am pressed against a brick wall
I don't know what words are but I would guess
they are the little hairs on my stomach that stand on end
when I know the future or when the future touches me
then leaves

#4

I'm not really dreaming. I'm in my room.
It is purple, with two windows, sparrow looking in.
Behind it, more birds flying into the duct and living
inside my walls. I hide them away with me. I hear them
at night. I don't tell the landlord, just the picture of
my grandfather hanging on the wall

#5

I'm not dreaming. I'm watching TV
and it watches me. Sings me a song right to left,
about a sparrow's cracked-whistle body. Broke its wings
before it broke from its jail. Had one song left.
A room with no windows.

#6

My grandfather waves to my grandmother
from the window he first saw her from.
Phonographs bloom from my eyes.
Sparrows at my shirtsleeves to carry me off
to where I'm really from   a phone, ringing.
Still ringing and there is no one listening, or
there is always someone listening.   I tell everyone.
I tell no one. I tell you.

Ghada says

never forget that softness is strength, unflinching
against the knife   and it is also the knife.

something uglier than a flower

my phone shows me the slaughter and my chest is a box caving in.
i want to unfold and offer myself to you. even now, as you don't want me.

my phone tells me the death of your matriarch is a point on the clock.
something expected. a nick in the sundial, waiting for shadow to fill the open
plot of it. we are all riddled with indents we can't see. we are all slowly buried alive
by light, or lack of it. skin that is and isn't ours.

but there she is, the slow crawl of genetics in the slope of your nose.
the gap in your teeth. the way you make a pact.

she carried your mother like a promise.
now, years later   a graze in your voice from the knife
held to the cord that fed you this magic.
no one sounds better than you

so talk to me about language again. tell me about the broken
collecting what it can in the grooves of itself so that
one day it may be more than a tongue.
what you would take from mine: i'll reveal
the jasmine you thought you lost.

did you ever ask about the roasting of pines?
the splintering of ships? the shrapnel left behind in gardens,
and the metal rod in my grandmother's arm?

you never asked, but here's everything i know about the hiding places.
the chicken shed when the militias came for the sons.
the space on the couch when the men came for the daughters.
dead sea flowing out of a mother dying in her son's arms,
black hole skull & bullet still six feet under a mountain somewhere,
waiting for me to leave flowers.

these are not gifts, they are buried artifacts.

my thighs could kill a man

they could snatch the lightning like a cigarette
from between zeus's fingers. they high five.
always stoked about something

my thighs meet each other like a prayer. i've got rosary beads
where bikes would have chains. they're dusty. rattling
like the ghost of christian past   but i like the way my scars
ooze hymnals. i hear them when middle eastern air filters
through the anise pods in my body.

and it's muffled, but when i walk i feel my great-grandmother's prayers
travel like sap through my tendons. the bullet that went through her head
is nestled between two lives i don't remember, but my thighs do
they're probably older than i am

every body part i have must have belonged to a dead relative,
all this biology that civil war failed to claim,   instead left us
with moles and hairs like constellations, connected   but less precious
my thighs, sleeping   on the capacity to kill with the roots stored
in the nucleus of me: that planet that centers all the rings.

give me the flute & sing

origin is an apple   jam jarred to make wine,
put in the ground but always comes up vinegar
when picked at the skin of where the earth
spit you out before you were you
but after the flute started playing.

hands are the etymology of prayer
i turn mine slowly in the morning sunlight
through my window. i watch the rings hug
my fingers. my knuckle hairs grow back
slower now, but i still have this inheritance
from a man who sang to his fig trees
and raised his voice at a woman sprung
from the shadow   of a tree full of switches

and all i can ever do is brew coffee for the
mild-mannered   and write stories
that don't belong to me

i come from love that didn't always know the right way.

a cracked seed aware of its cyanide. bruised fruit.
preserves or vinegar, depending on the light.

his body pushes up tomatoes
wherever her hands waver.   this too,
a type of apology i listen for
until that flute in me stops.

ahwak

the whole world
comes with you

                              i no longer
                                  believe
                               it leaves
                                   when
                                you do.

notepad fragments

i am always searching for the moon. maybe
instead of blood, i am full of moths.

أنت القمر في حياتي
you're the moon of my life

summer solstice: when fireflies hatch from the empty wombs of bullet cases
when everything is softer unfolding from the tree trunk dusk of the throat,
      i wonder
how many times has arabic let
a lover down easy?

        last night i had tears in my eyes for jido
        but for the first time in months they were
        of laughter
he wrote ghazals & still lives
in their meter somewhere on the wind.
i want everyone to be honest about their longing, to face it where it lives
        in the space between losses
        the only space we get.

one day i will write a ghazal
when it stops feeling like
a wind tunnel

الزهور تتفتح على لسانك
flowers bloom on your tongue
    the last few people i cried about will never know
the alternative(s):

i am two paper cranes

        i hand you one of them   you smile

        but do not extend your hand

        you do not water my plants when i am gone

        all the windows closed,

ذبول اسمي في فمك

my name wilting in your mouth

i sing like grackles do under the high notes of bulbuls

i ride the coattails of their stories   at dusk when the fireflies

distract you from my ankles

        so i keep singing.

a room with no wind   i just

        want you

        to know   i love you

        forgive me.

origin story

i was born to refugees,
i was named a miracle   still, they wait
for something greater.

i'm alive, and therefore enough.

i have space for an extra organ
that never came home
and every year the sea levels rise.

Or   i have a twin that never followed me out of the womb,
is still stuck where a shrieking echo
comes down on a mountain village   and the telepathy between us
is a gold thread so warm, it hums.

i'll never know its language   older than the polaroids
falling out of my mothers mouth   older than the lute
in my father's whistle

or   mama gave birth to me & i came out a hyphen
i was born the big hand on a clock

or   i was born an arm with a hand at both ends
taking both lands back at once, like they're mine

i was born an arm   with a hand at both ends
holding a knife   maybe i am a knife,
always spinning   slicing

at roots and fruits i graft into the hollow
where the ancient humming organ
never made its home.

maybe i am this organ myself.
maybe this organ will be my country,
& everyone i love
is safe here.

Ghada says

when your hands have handled enough
ovens and hot pans and wax, they will stop
feeling the burn.

you will be able to touch the sun
in all the hiding places it keeps around you:
the summer chain links   thrown over the ocean
the door of your car   the whites of his eyes, one day
your hands won't be soft,
i hope they are always soft   i hope to god
                    you bury me

i am a garden of bones but don't call me a cemetery

in his dreams my father lights candles for
a dead man who once shared our blood

a single flicker to light a dark room,
this silent whistle he holds in his fingers
& uses to light cigarettes.
    a morning ritual makes the turkish coffee smoother
& smokes out the swallow in him that repeats his dreams
into the muddy porcelain.   these grounds might be his future.

the cup readers tell us to stamp a thumb into the grounds,
now let yourself want, now lick this future from your finger
and this must be how you look for God inside of dirt
before you're fed to it
    and when we are   we push the worms of us back up
like fingers reaching for heaven.

we were always much closer to the ground than we thought,
our lives spent learning to speak both in bird song
and elegy. anise root
and burnt cedar.

the man in the ground once said   be the balsam
to the serpent's venom   be as sweet as another's bitterness

the man in the ground once said   America is responsible
for every child   who falls asleep crying.

now my America responsible for holding his body down
while he died, now holds it like a breath.
i still hear his whistle in my fingers when I stop
to touch flowers.

listen   when I am gone, stamp the ashes of me
like a thumb into the ground. I want to be petals
between your fingers   something soft
to stick into the barrel of their gun.

NOTES

in *there goes the family* the quote from Merchant of Venice is slightly rearranged.

the song referenced in section #5 of "dream log" is *Asfour* by Marcel Khalife.

give me the flute & sing was written in response to Khalil Gibran's poem as performed by Fairouz.

ahwak was written after Abdelhalim Hafez's song of the same name.

notepad fragments was arranged after Ocean Vuong's *notebook fragments*.